Copyright

Introduction

Welcome to Volume Three of my Manga stylized coloring book series!

This time I focused on villains. I wanted to make it pretty diverse so you will find evil characters in various styles, not necessarily from one universe. There are some gang animals, mafia bosses and even supervillains.

I hope that you will like it and share your thoughts about this book with me. This is the last Manga styled book for now as I think with three books already, I saturated the market for a while. Still, there is a kawaii theme in my mind but we will see.

Sincerely, Slavo Mirro

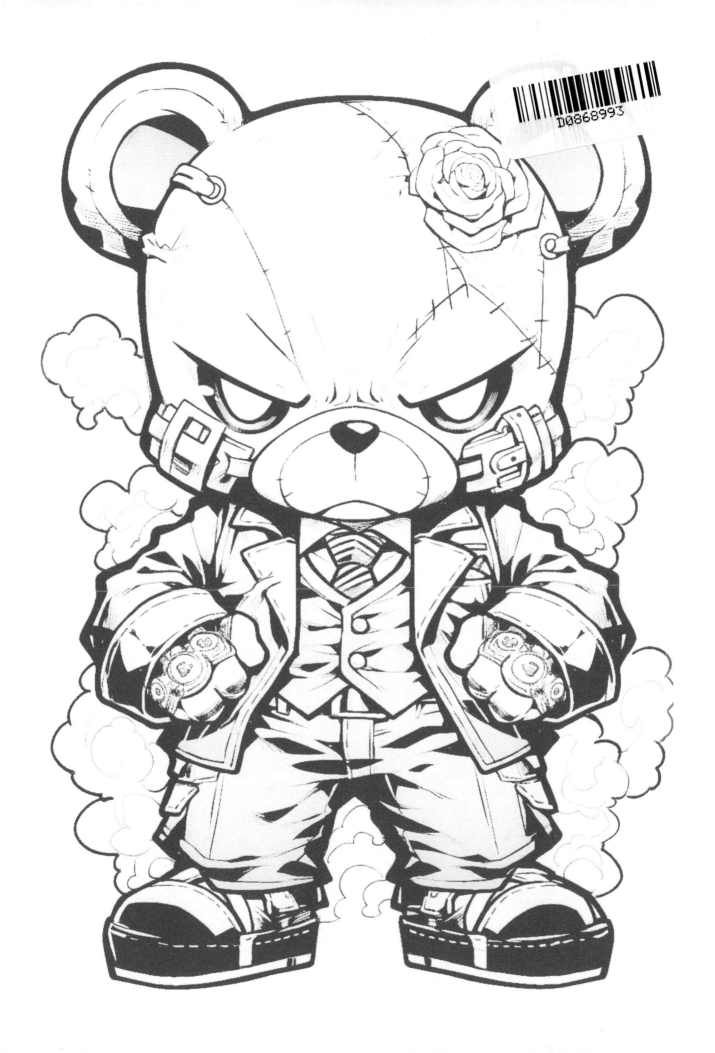

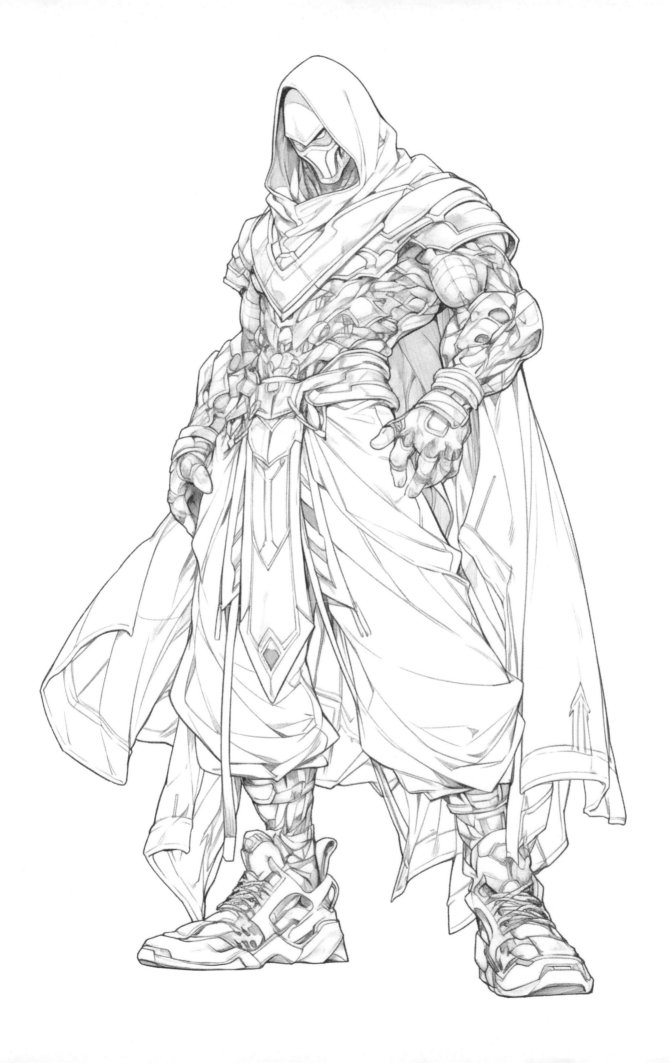

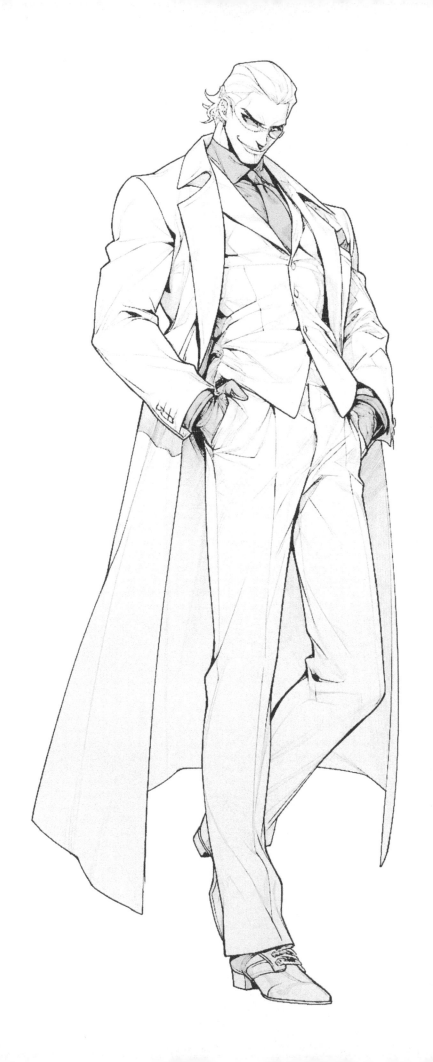

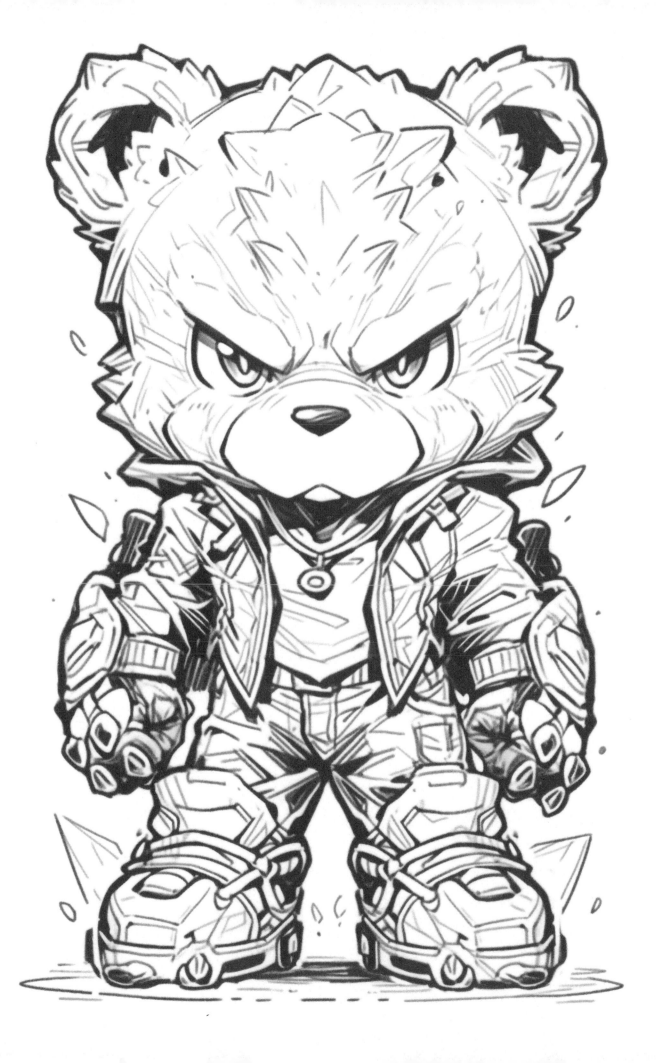

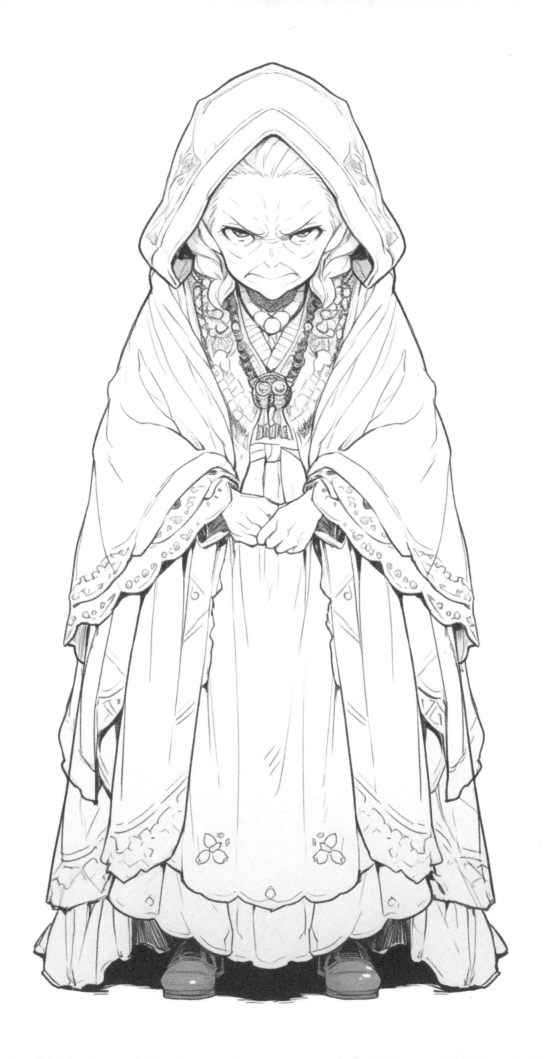

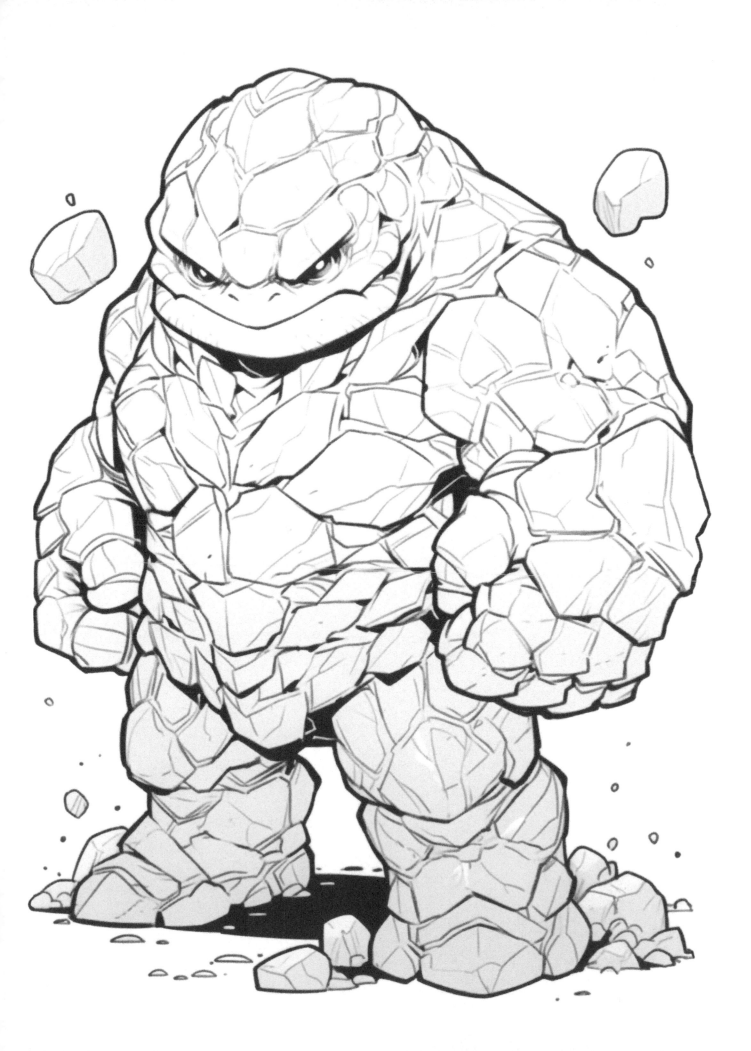

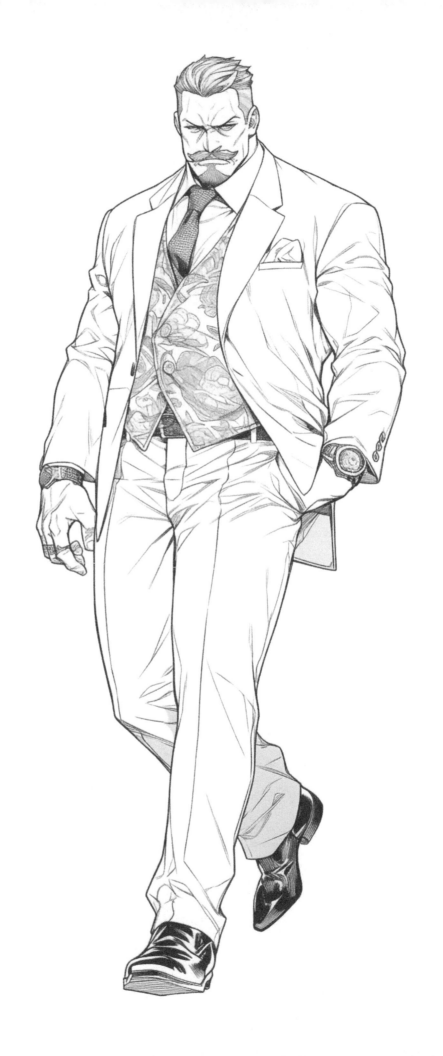

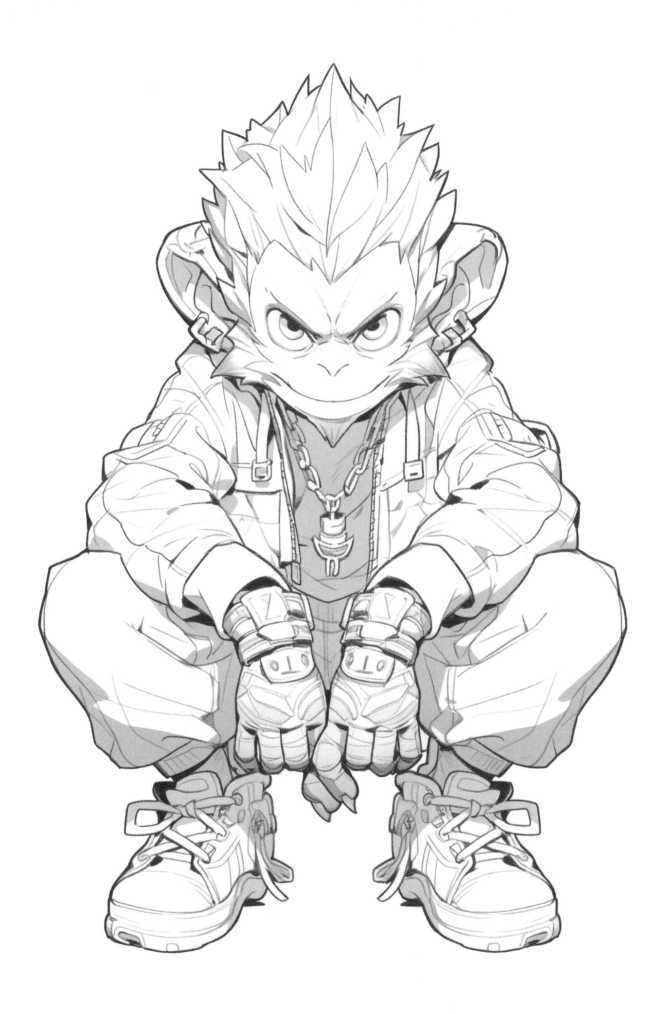

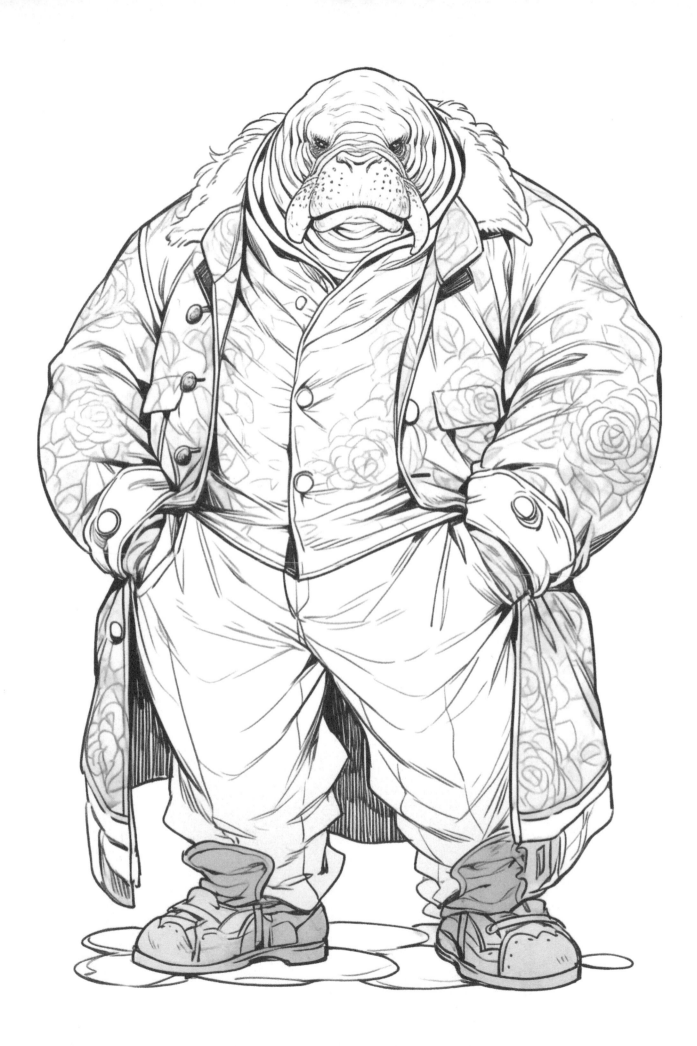

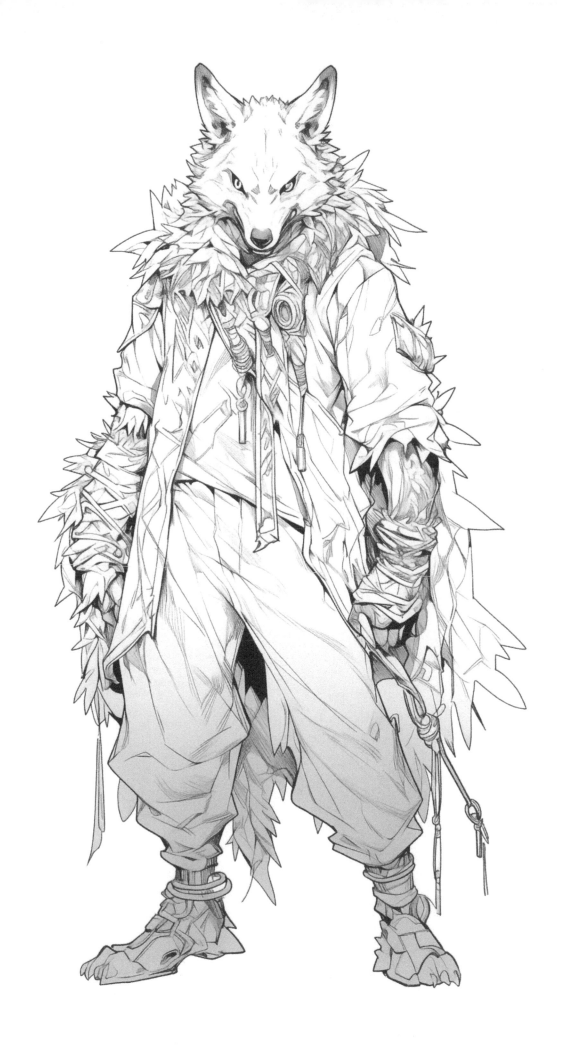

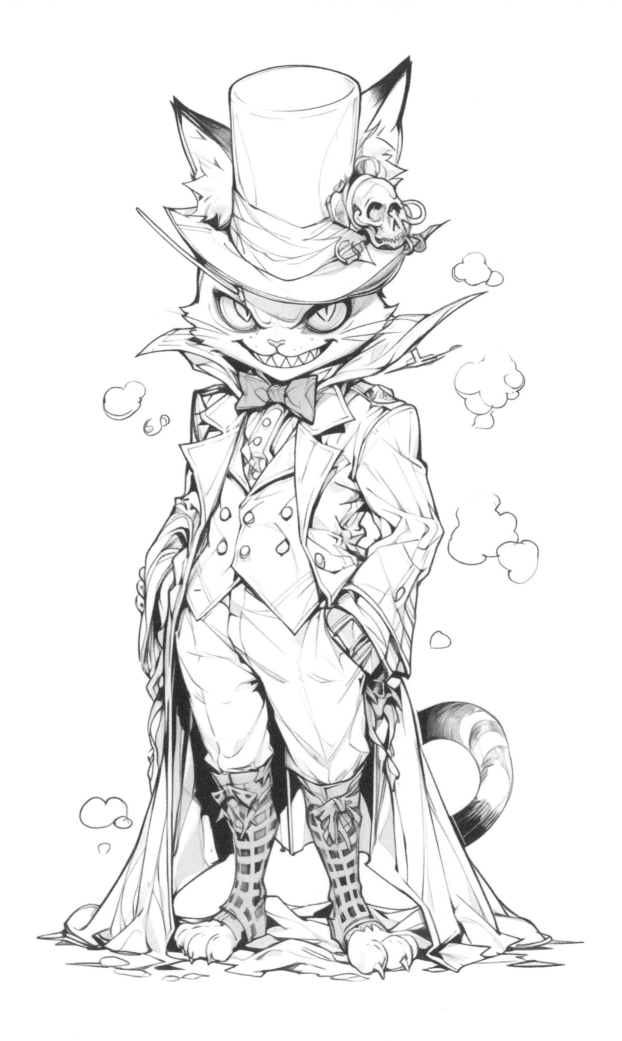

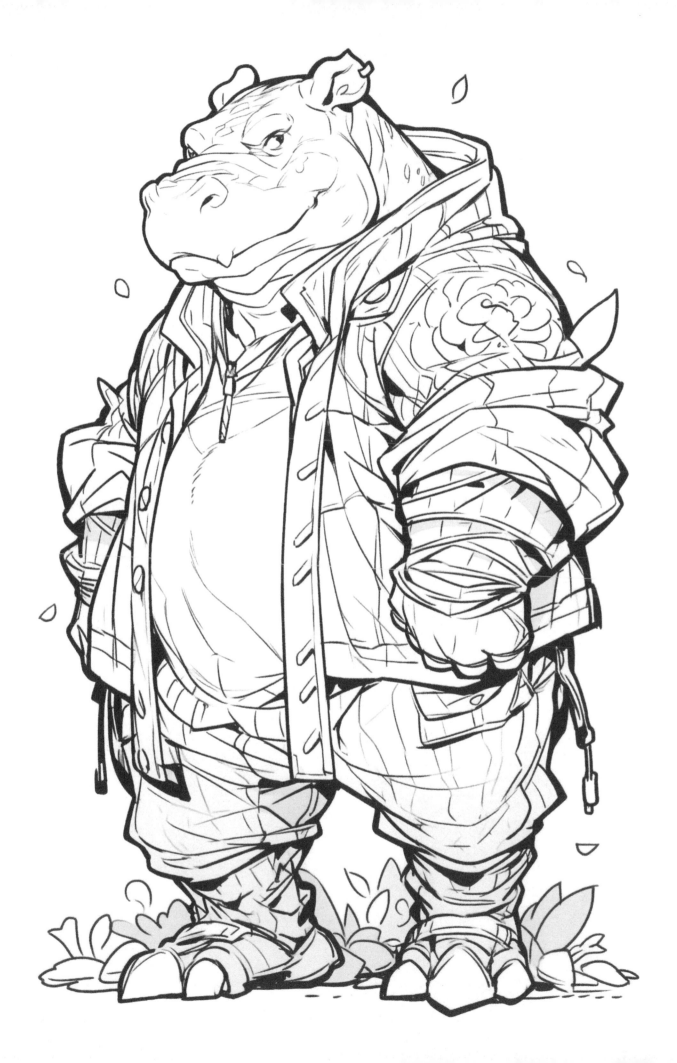

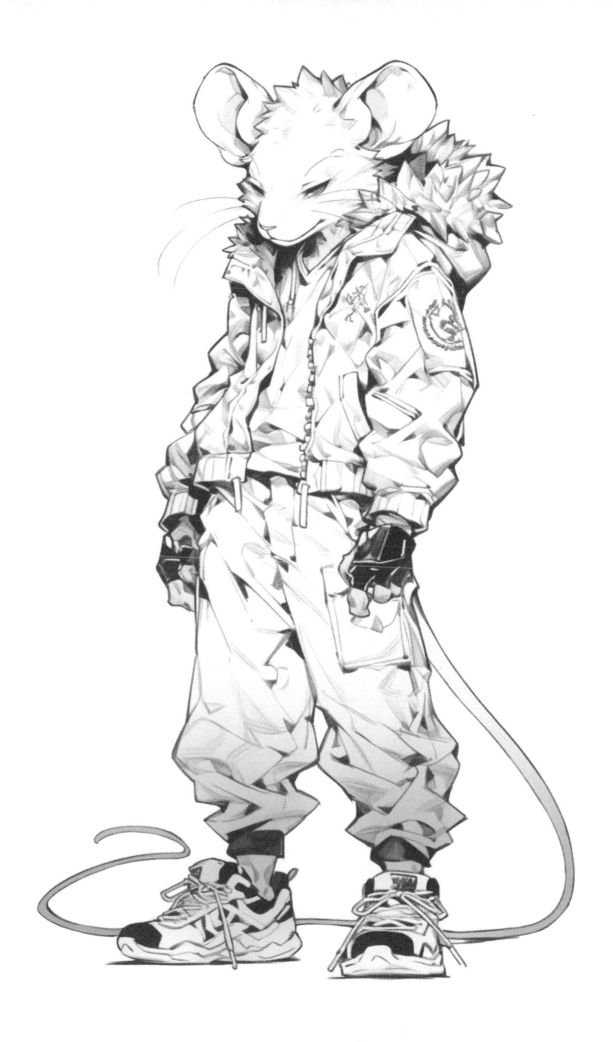

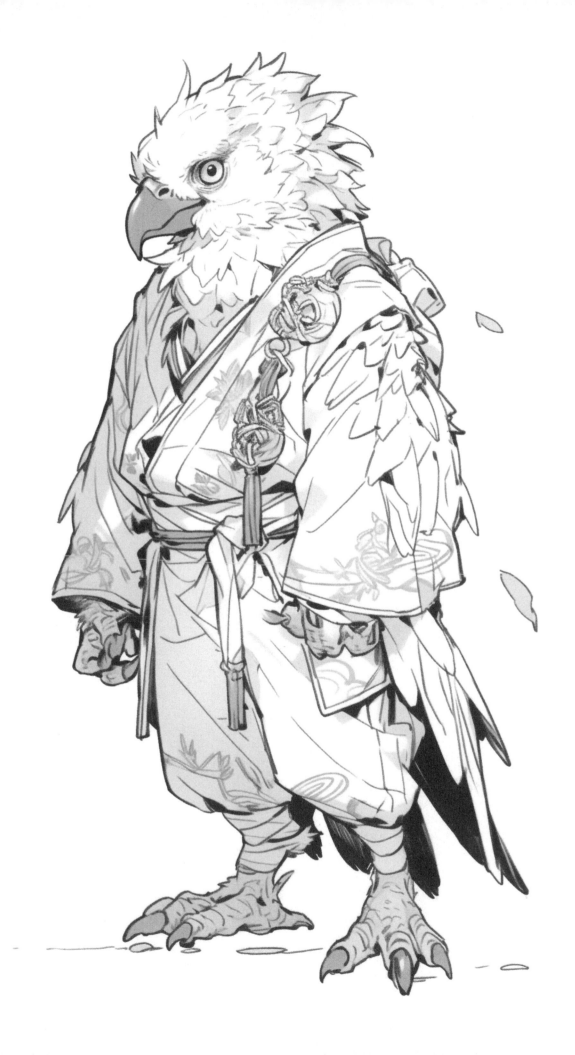

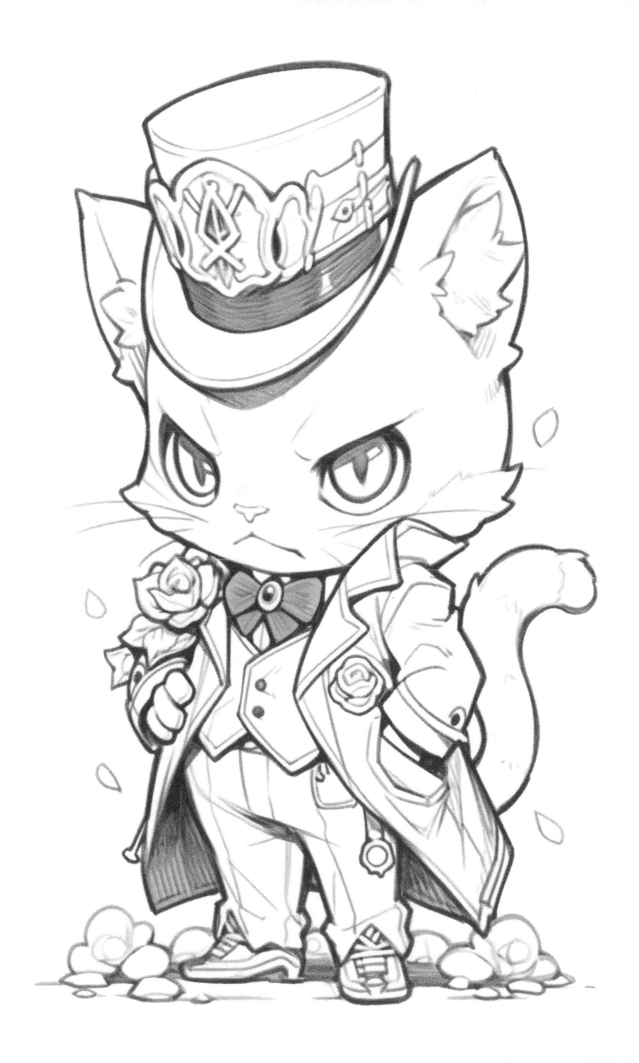

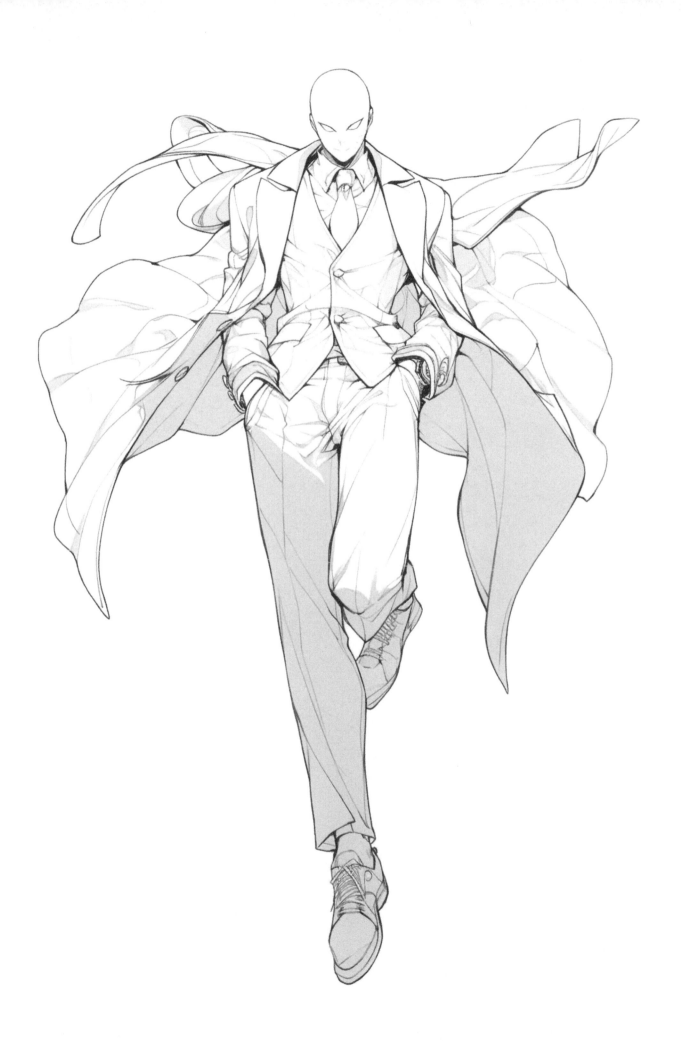

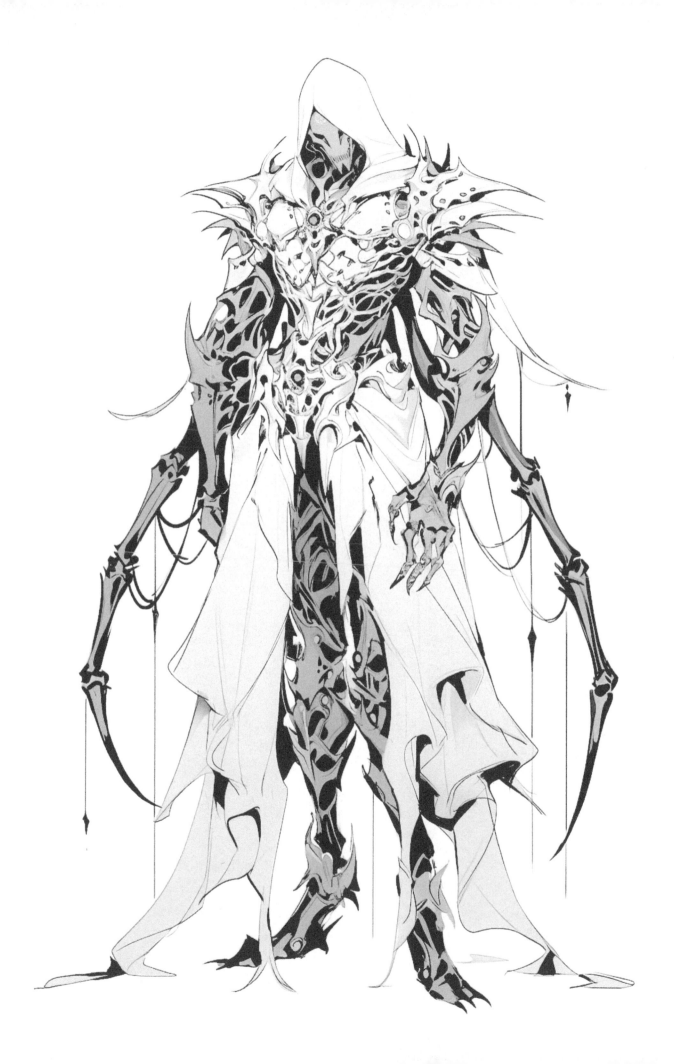

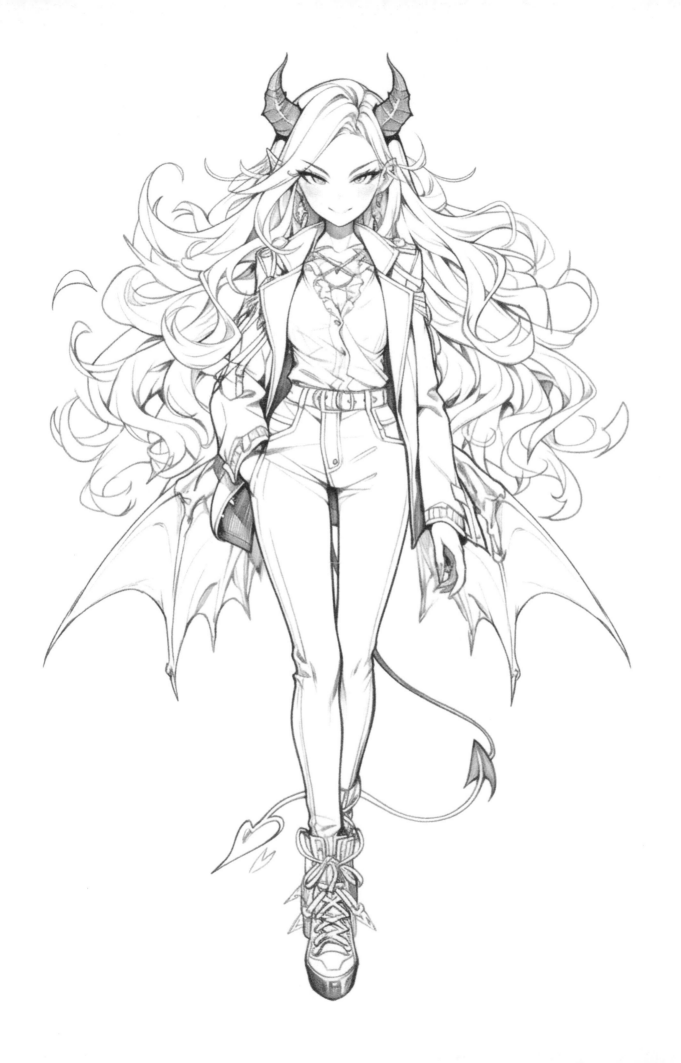

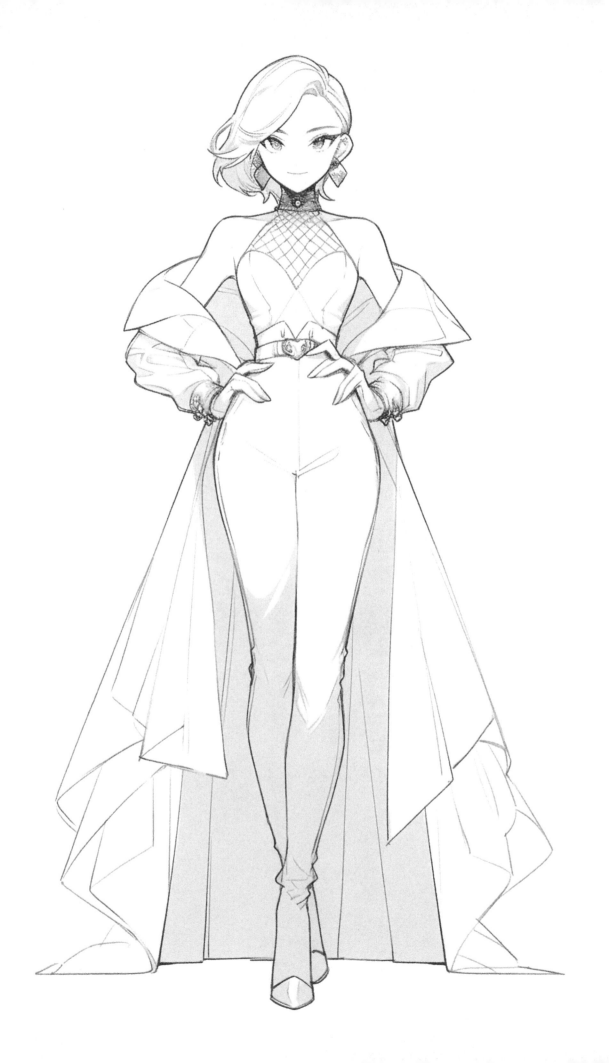

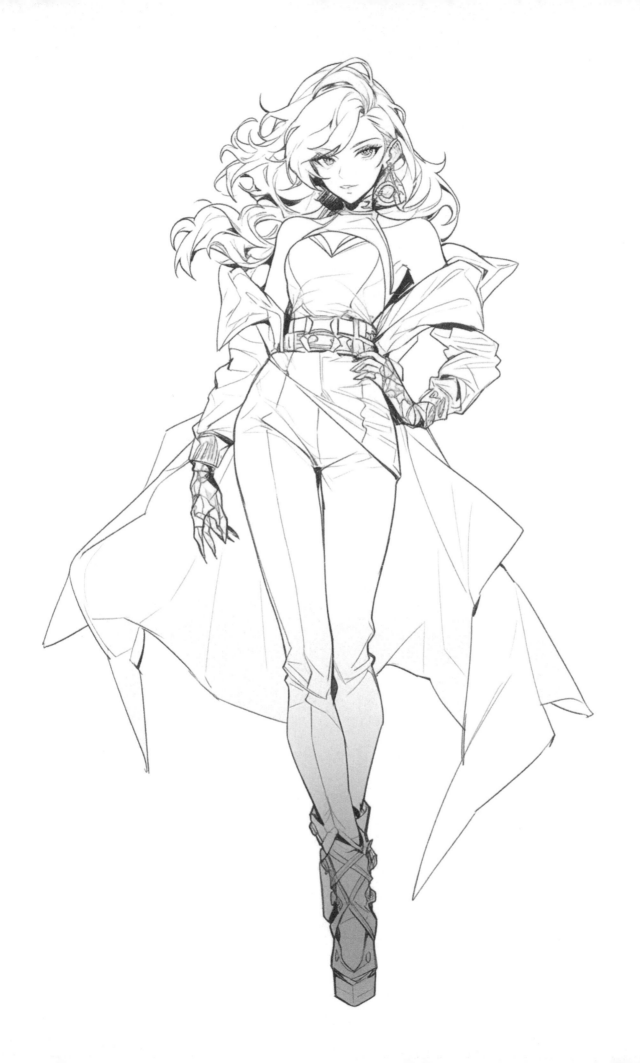

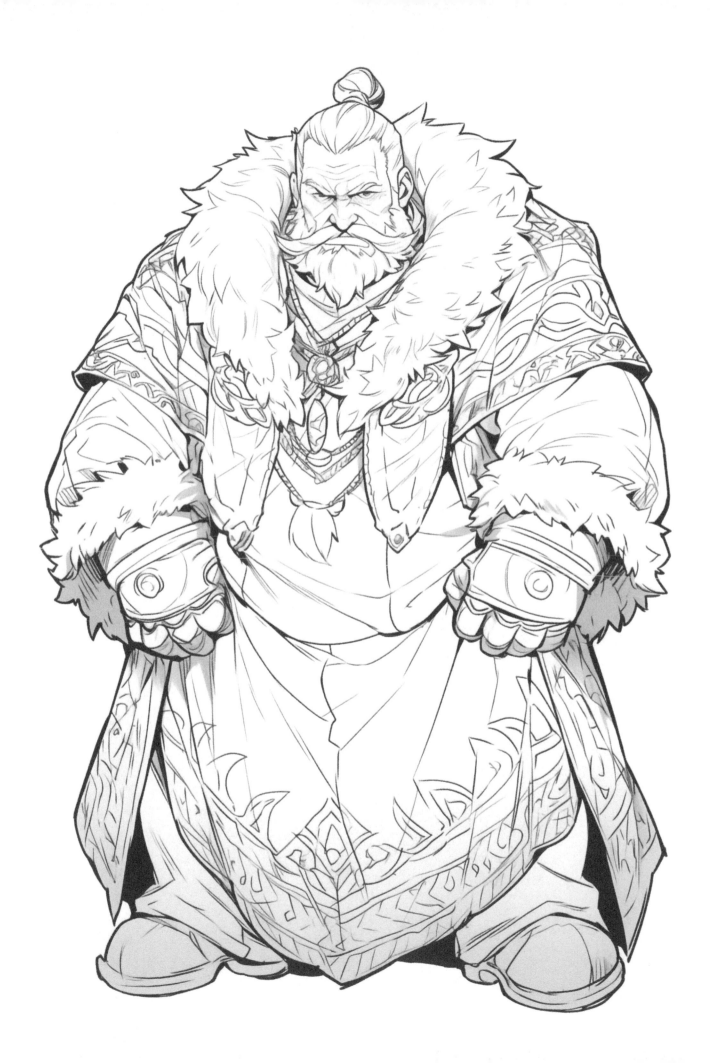

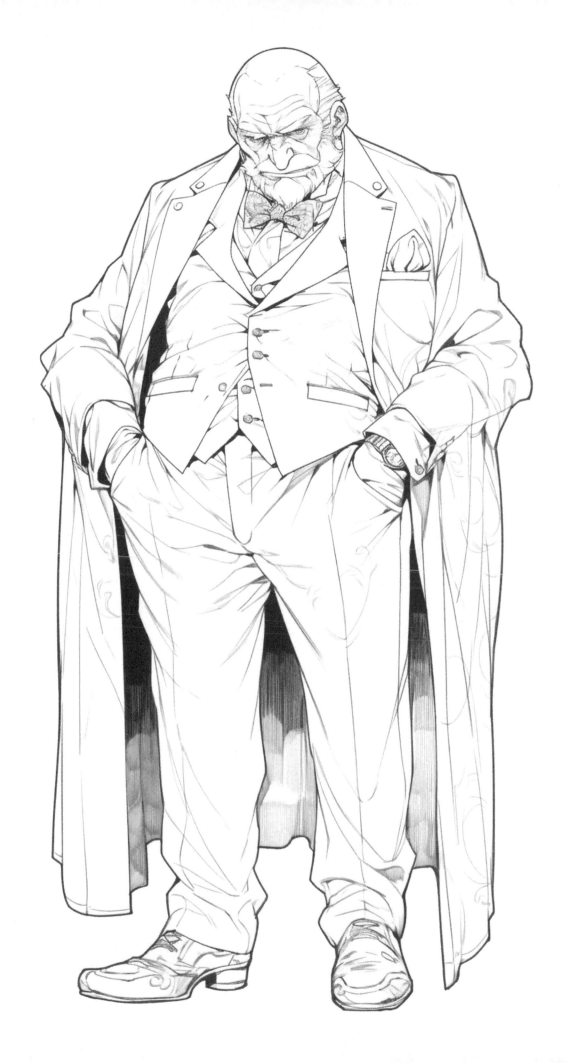

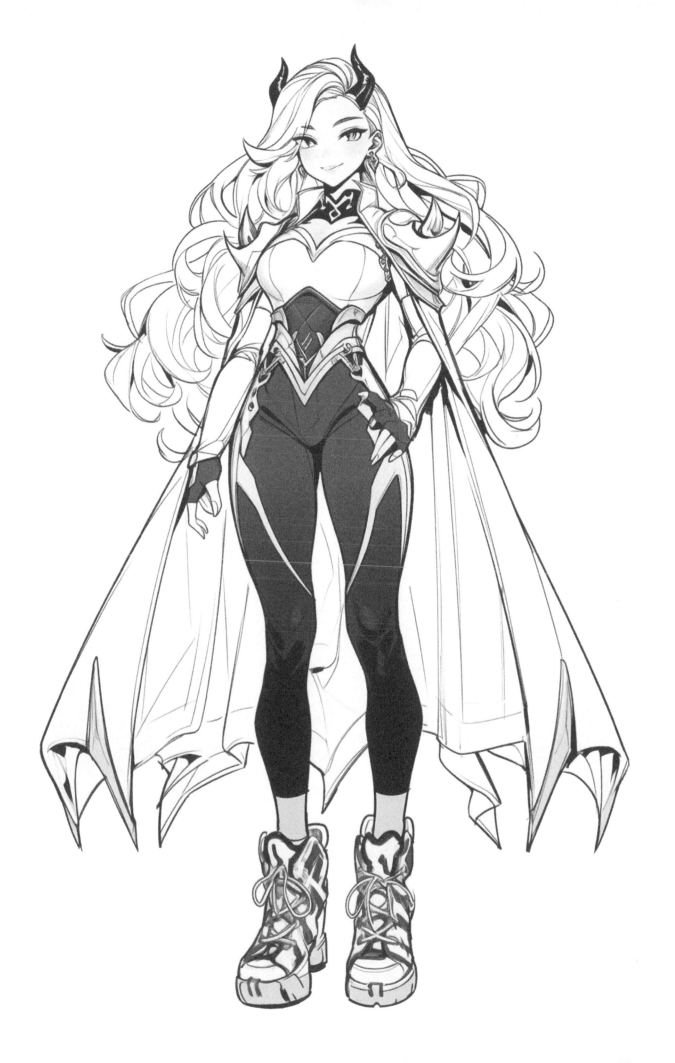

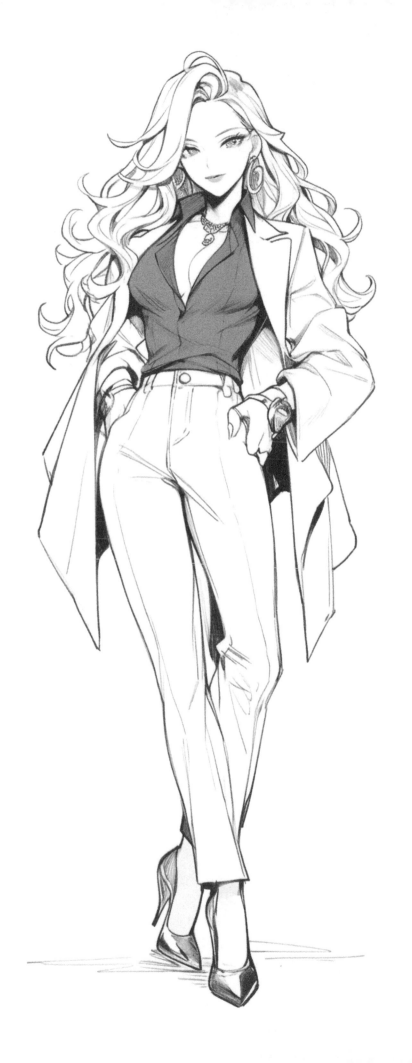

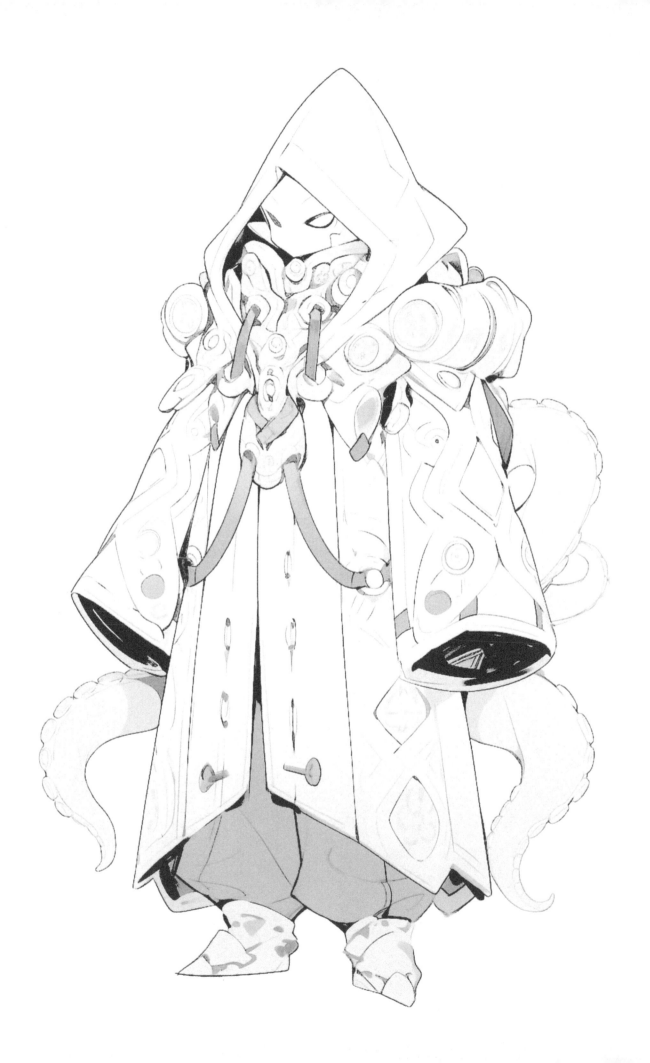

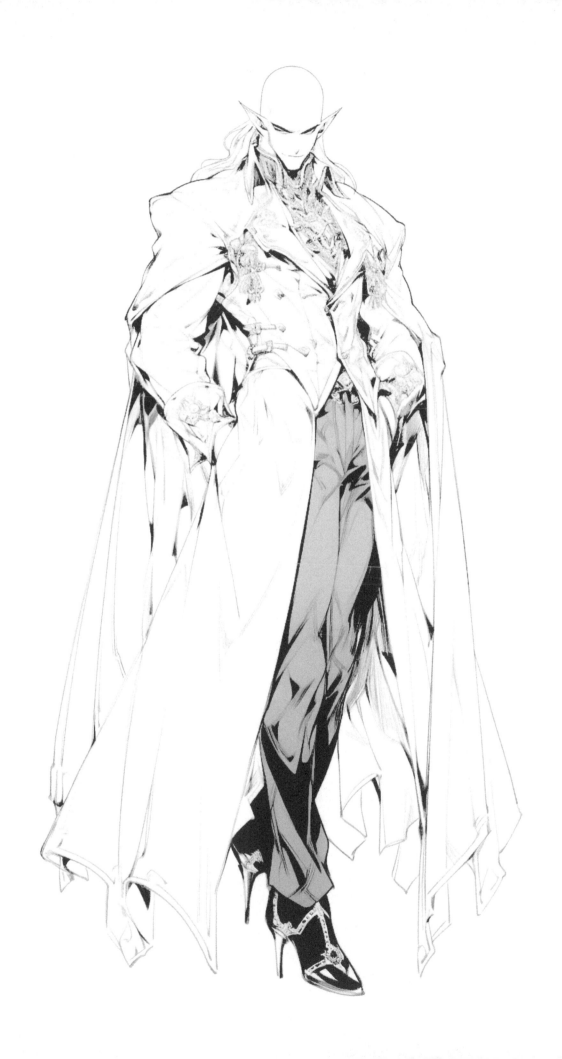

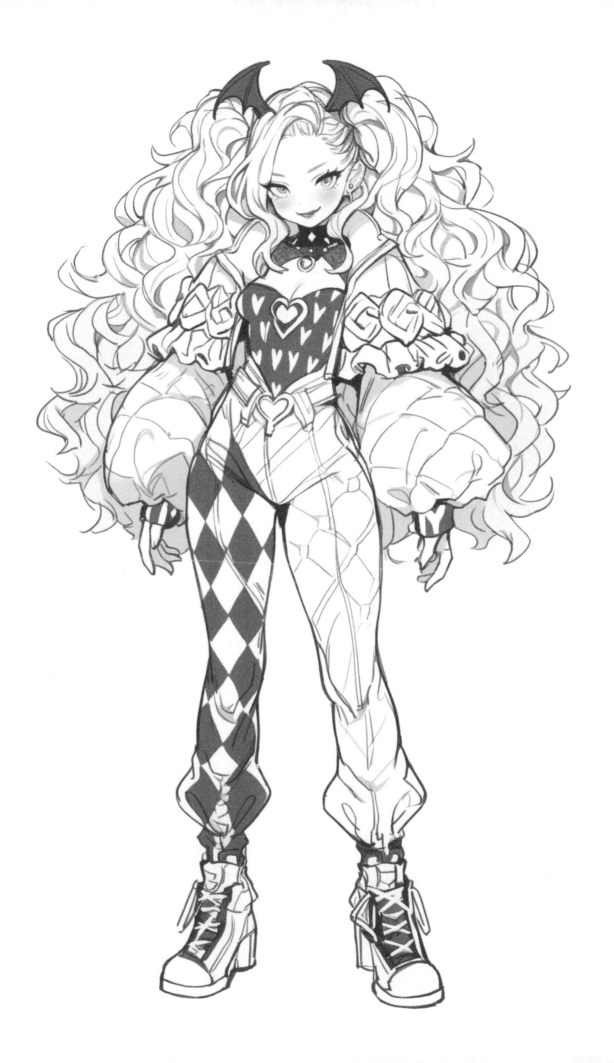

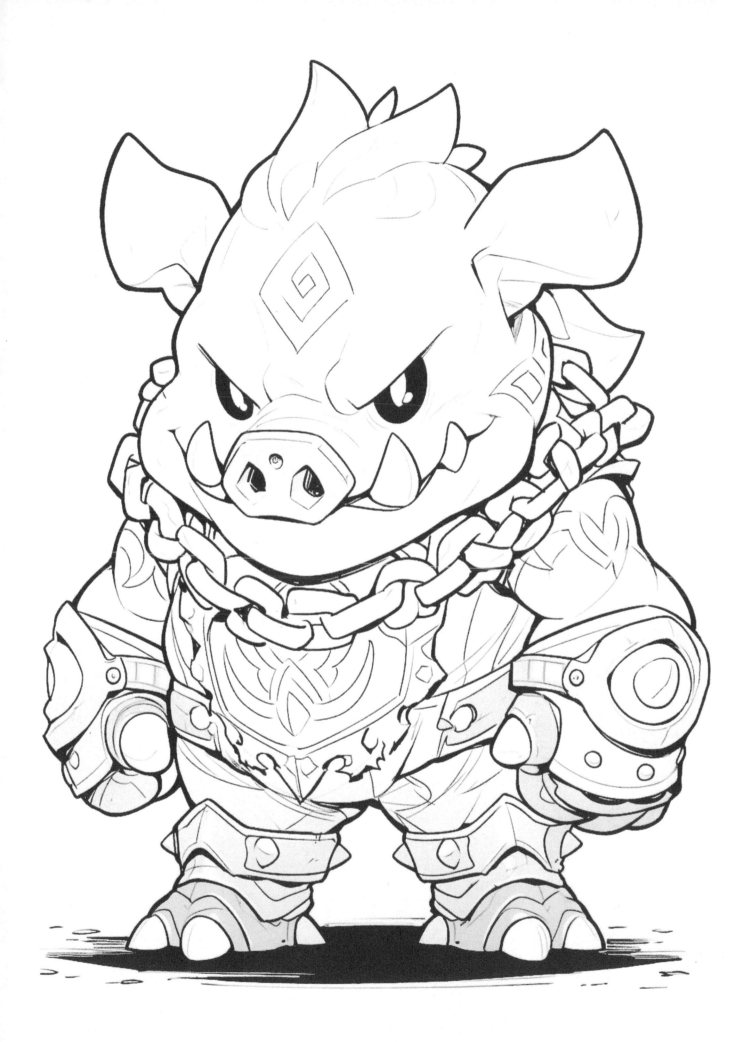

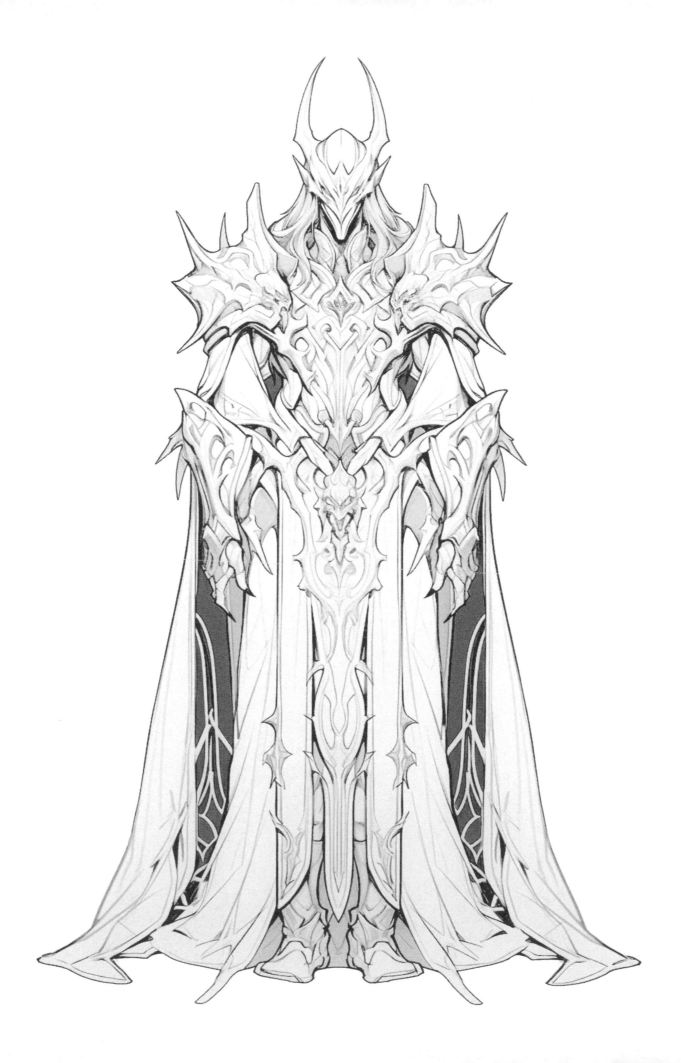

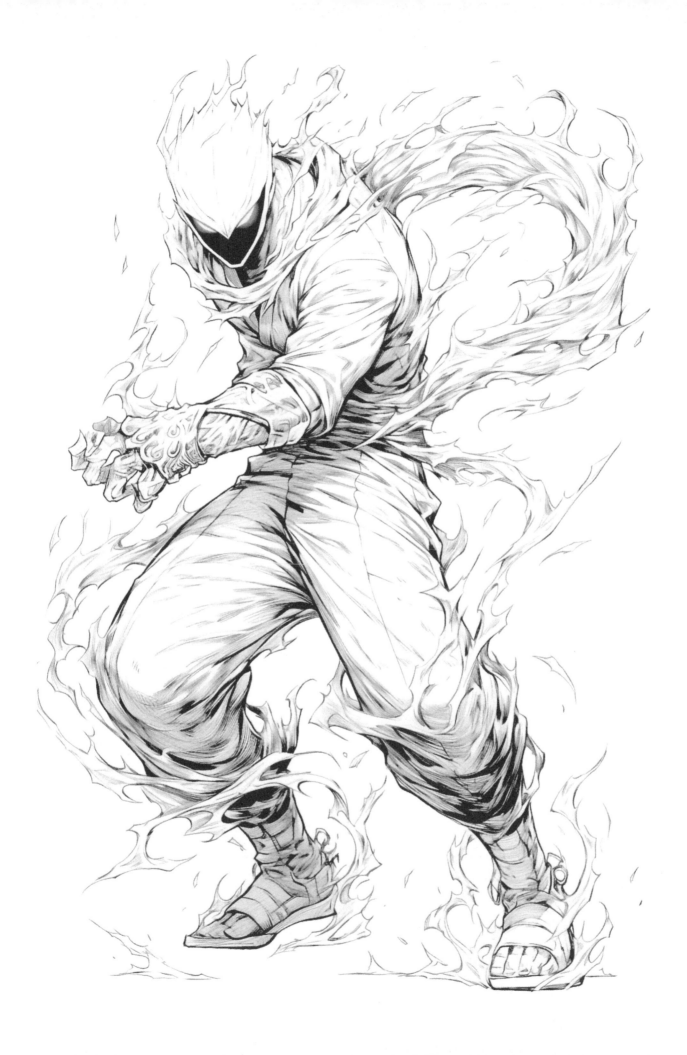

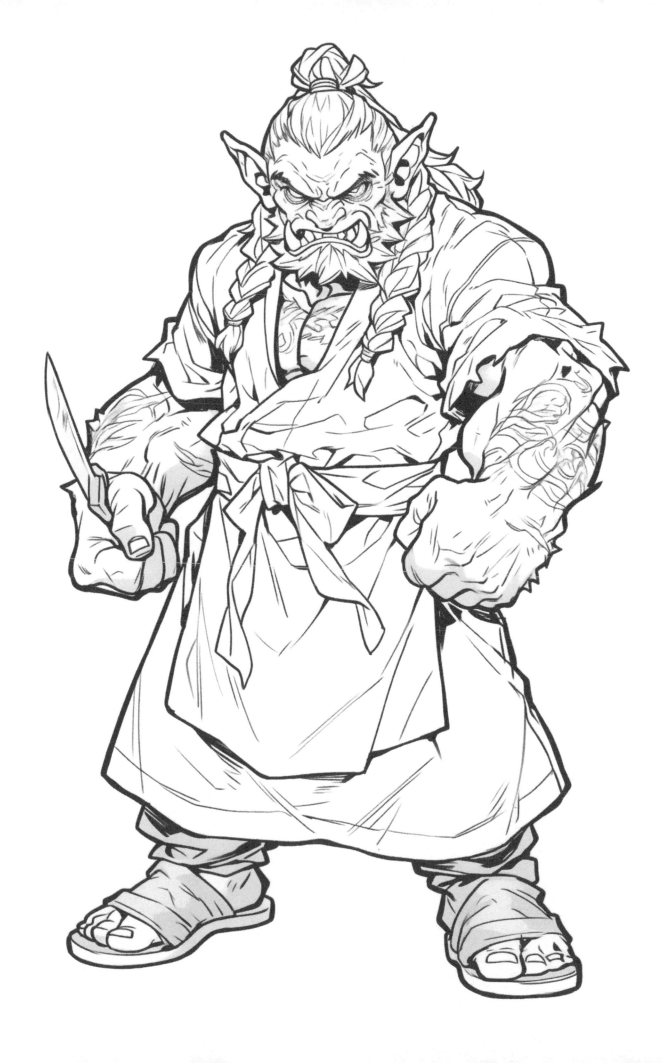

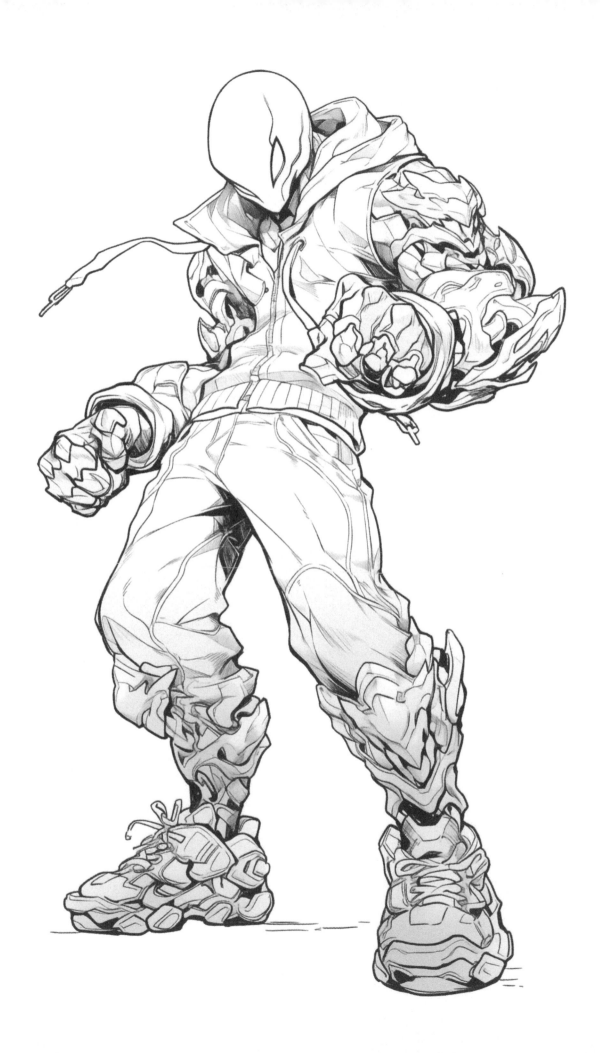

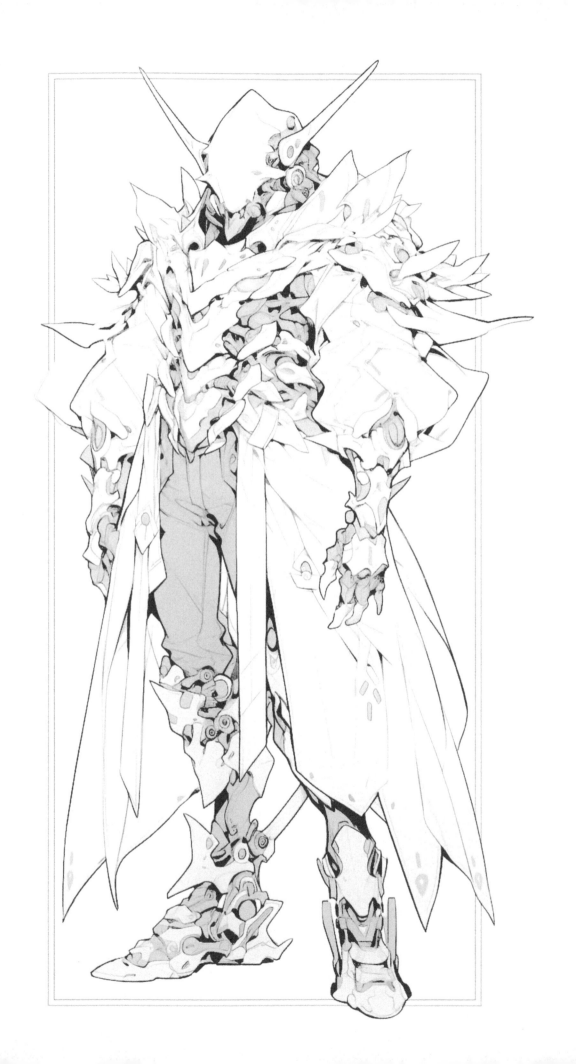

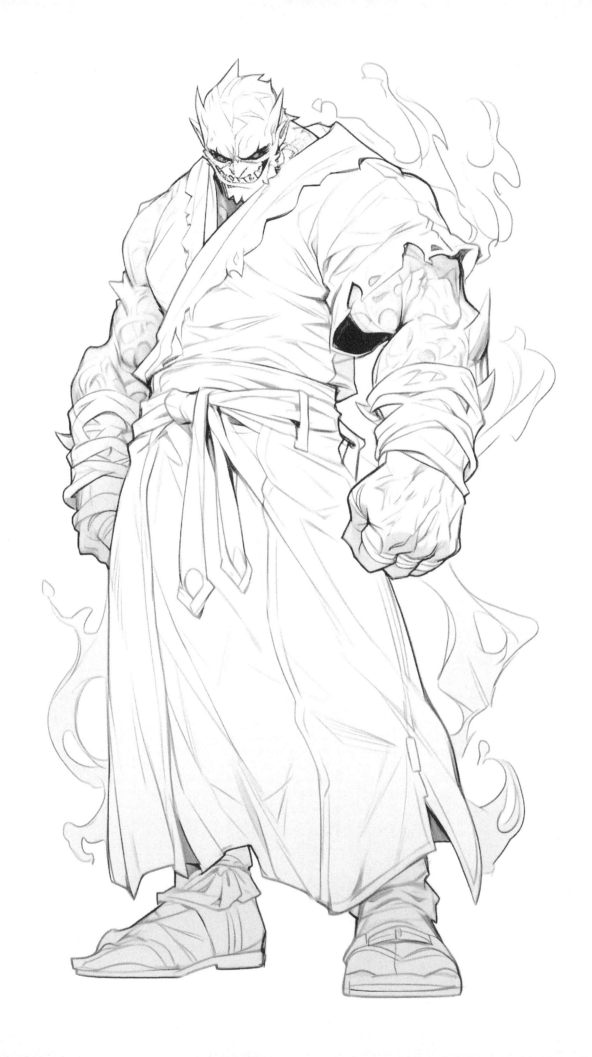

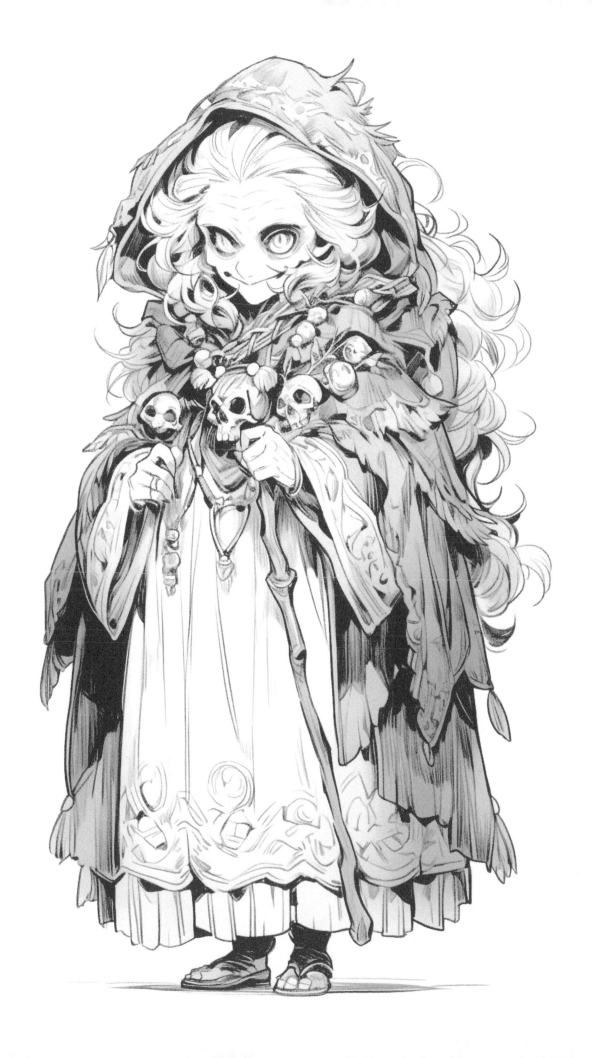

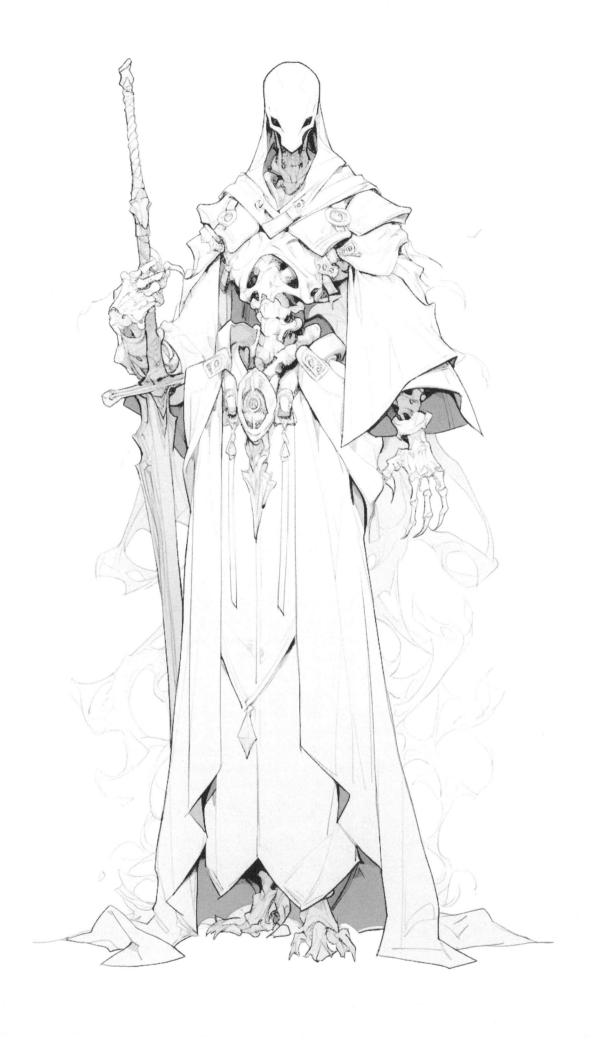

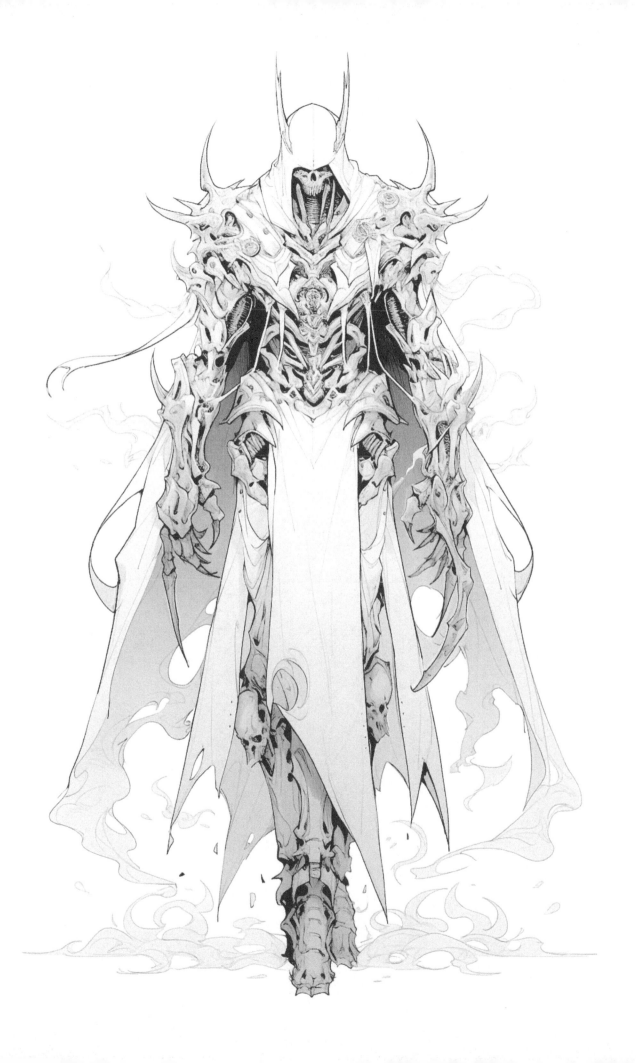

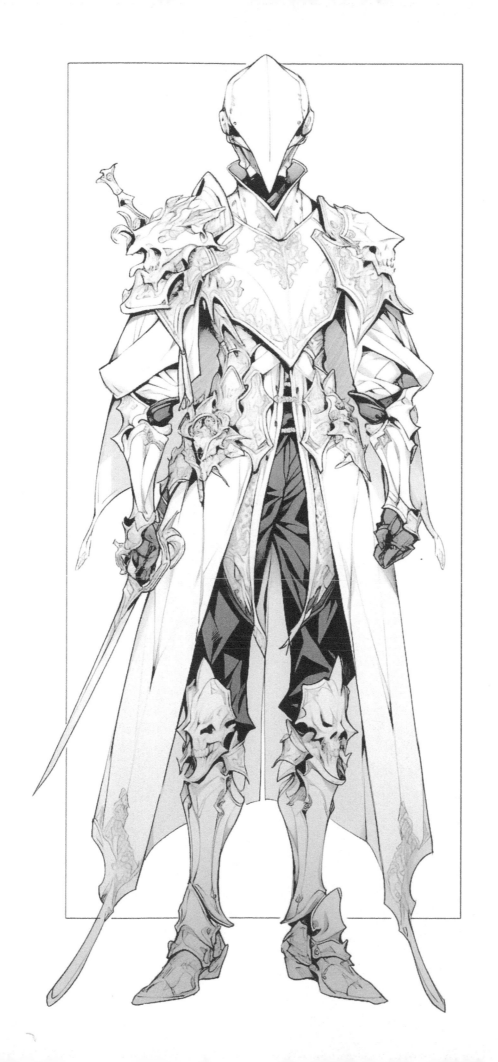

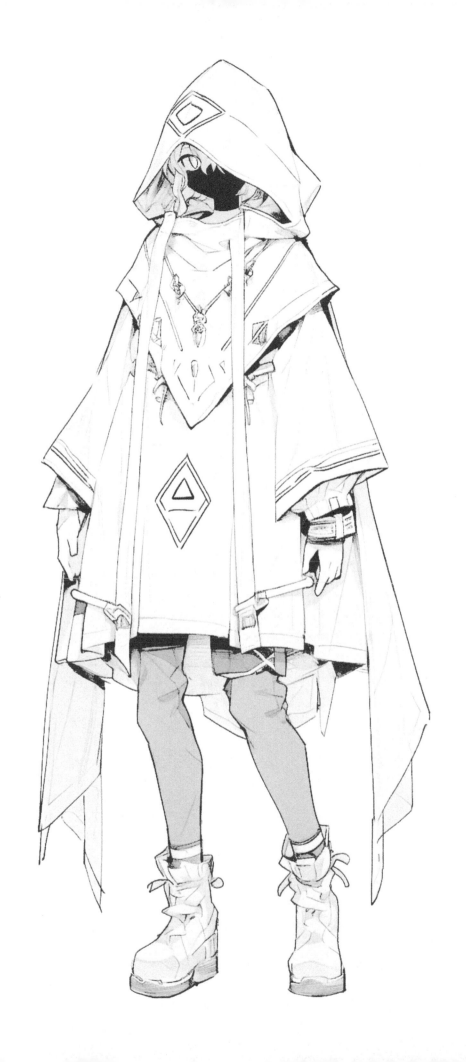

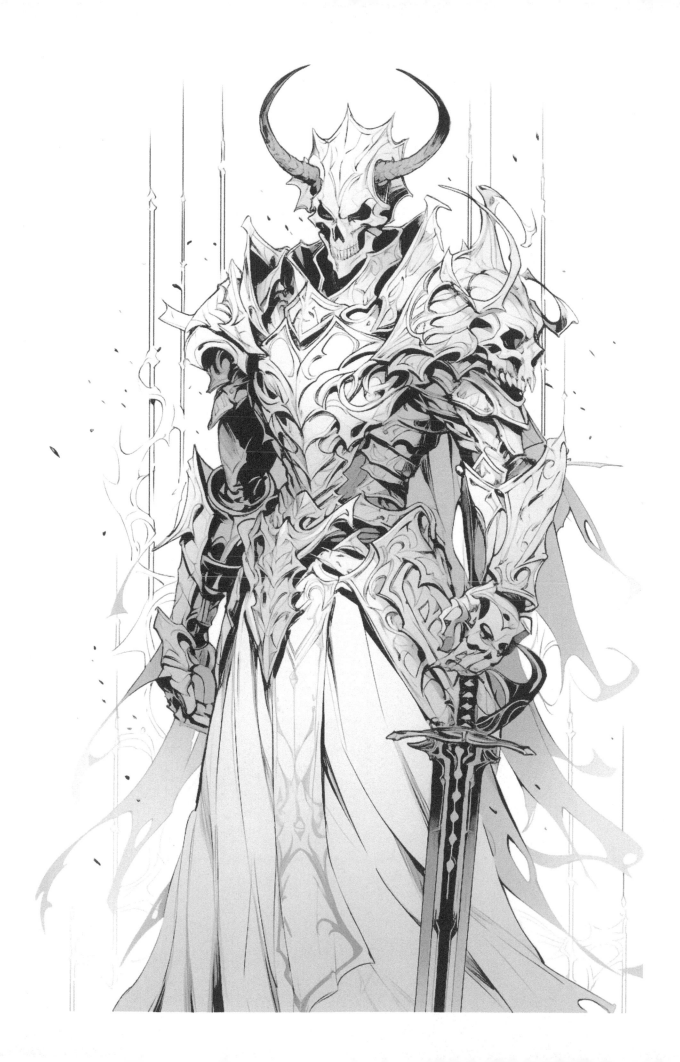